Penny Stocks

How to Invest and Trade Penny Stocks Like a Pro to Maximize Your Gains and Reduce Your Risks

by David Berman

Copyright 2018 Beryl Assets LLC - All rights reserved worldwide.

Published simultaneously in Canada.

Disclaimer: This document is designed to provide accurate and authoritative information in regard to the subject matter covered. It is offered with the understanding that the presenters are not engaged in rendering legal, accounting, or other professional service. If legal advice or other expert advice is required, the services of a competent professional should be sought.

Adapted from a Declaration of Principles which was accepted and approved equally by a Committee of the American Bar Association and a Committee of Publishers and Associations.

The information provided herein is stated to be truthful and consistent, in that any liability, in terms of inattention or otherwise, by any usage or abuse of any policies, processes, or directions contained within is the solitary and utter responsibility of the recipient reader. This information has been obtained from sources believed to be reliable. The author made diligent efforts to ensure accuracy, however it is stressed that the information is provided with no guarantee (1) of accuracy, (2) of absence of error or (3) of absence of omission. You should always verify any and all information through your own sources.

Under no circumstances will any legal responsibility or blame be held against the publisher, the author or Beryl Assets LLC (hereafter and together the "presenters") for any reparation, damages, or monetary loss due to the information provided in this book, either directly or indirectly.

The information presented in this book represents only the opinion of the author as of the date of its publication.

Respective authors own all copyrights not held by the publisher.

The information herein is offered for general information purposes solely, and is universal as so. This book does not provide complete information on the subject matter and cannot, as such, be used as a sole source of information. The presentation of the information is without contract or any type of guarantee assurance. No information contained in this book constitutes investment, tax, legal, stock, equity or insurance advice. This book should not be considered either as communicating an invitation to engage in investment activities. You should determine your own investment decisions and strategies based on your own judgment and on your personal and specific financial circumstances. You should also keep in mind that investments can result in a loss and understand that you should always consult a competent professional before taking any investment decision and before putting any funds at risk.

LIMIT OF LIABILITY/DISCLAIMER OF WARRANTY: WHILE THE PUBLISHER AND AUTHOR HAVE USED THEIR BEST EFFORTS IN PREPARING THIS BOOK, THEY MAKE NO REPRESENTATIONS OR WARRANTIES WITH RESPECT TO THE ACCURACY OR COMPLETENESS OF THE CONTENTS OF THIS BOOK AND SPECIFICALLY DISCLAIM ANY IMPLIED WARRANTIES OF MERCHANTABILITY OR FITNESS FOR A PARTICULAR PURPOSE. NO WARRANTY MAY BE CREATED OR EXTENDED BY SALES REPRESENTATIVES OR WRITTEN SALES MATERIALS. THE ADVICE AND STRATEGIES CONTAINED HEREIN MAY NOT BE SUITABLE

FOR YOUR SITUATION. YOU SHOULD CONSULT WITH A PROFESSIONAL WHERE APPROPRIATE. NEITHER THE PUBLISHER NOR THE AUTHOR SHALL BE LIABLE FOR DAMAGES ARISING THEREFROM.

Any stocks mentioned in this book are for illustrative and educational purposes only. Under no circumstances does it imply that you should invest in these stocks nor that they could be appropriate for you. It's the reader's responsibility to conduct his own due diligence and to make his own decisions.

The trademarks that are used are without any consent, and the publication of the trademark is without permission or backing by the trademark owner. All trademarks and brands within this book are for clarifying purposes only and are owned by their respective owners. Beryl Assets LLC and the Author are not associated nor affiliated with any product, vendor or trademark owner mentioned in this book.

Companies mentioned are for example and illustrative purpose only. No company is endorsed or recommended. Just ideas, for you to decide if it's right for you after seeking the assistance of a competent and appropriate professional: lawyer, accountant, financial advisor, mortgage broker or else. The author, the publisher and Beryl Assets LLC do not provide any legal or other professional advice.

With respect to any third-party website or company mentioned in this book the reader is hereby prompted to read and acknowledge their respective terms and conditions before using them. The presenters assume no responsibility whatsoever in connection with their use.

All right reserved: No part of this book may be reproduced or utilized in any form or by any means, electronic or mechanical, including photocopying, recording or by any information storage and retrieval system, or distributed without permission in writing of Beryl Assets LLC. In no way is it legal to reproduce, duplicate, translate or transmit any part of this document in either electronic means or in printed format. Recording of this publication is strictly prohibited and any storage of this document is not allowed unless with written permission from the publisher. All rights reserved.

Table of Contents

Introduction	1
What are Penny Stocks?	7
An Introduction to OTCBB	19
What are the SEC rules for Penny Stocks?	25
The Four Penny Stock Levels	35
Where to Trade in Penny Stocks?	43
How to Trade in Penny Stocks?	53
Trading Tips	61
Risks and Manipulations	79
An example of Penny Stock Fraud	89
Conclusion	95
Check Out My Other Books	99
Bonus	101

Introduction

Welcome to 'Penny Stocks: how to invest and trade penny stocks like a pro to maximize your gains and reduce your risks.' The concept of this book was born after being approached several times by coworkers, friends or family members about investing in penny stocks and out of the necessity to understand penny stock trading as an alternative or addition to other acceptable trading platforms.

Who Am I?

I am an investor who is conscious about growing his portfolio and managing his assets in the most efficient way possible. I invest in various instruments such as real estate and stocks. I started out trading as most investors do, with basics of the stock exchange, NYSE, NASDAQ, etc. Then I got a bit more speculative and started trading options, not binary, but stock options traded on the same exchanges. After this, I realized that there was so much more to learn to maximize my earnings such as Forex and Cryptocurrencies. On my way, through my years of trading education, I also started touching penny stocks, and they opened my eyes to many interesting scenarios.

What Makes Penny Stocks a Different Type of Investment?

Penny stocks are speculative instruments by nature, even so, they are better than cryptocurrencies because they are based on actual companies, with real values. At the same time, they can be difficult to trade in since trading can be static, which is something we will look at later in this book. Due to the unusual nature of the penny stock trading platform, these assets can become highly volatile, so understanding how to trade in them is key to success.

Is This Book Right For You?

This book has been designed for new investors and for experienced investors who are new to penny stocks as well. This is not a book from a stock broker, but from an individual investor to other individual investors. It makes no unrealistic promise of millions of dollars in gains nor will it explains that there is a magic formula to follow to make the big bucks. However, what this book will do for you is to guide you through the basics that any penny stock investor must understand. I will discuss proven methods, accumulated from over 30 years of experience trading on various markets, including penny stocks, standard exchanges, forex and cryptocurrencies, as well as hands-on experience in raising funding from private equity for start-ups, running businesses and researching new models and concepts. I will go with you over the history of penny stocks, the regulations and trading platforms, and present tips and methods for successfully trading in penny stock assets.

I will conclude this introduction by quoting the world's leading investor, Warren Buffet: "Most failures are based on adhering to a good premise rather than a false one." The reason is due to the premise being sound but the person not being flexible. A premise can lead people to make static decisions that do not reflect what the market dynamics are pointing to. So, don't believe in something only because you are told it is so, question everything, and make an informed (and sometimes gut) decision.

I hope you enjoy this book and I truly wish you the best.

What are Penny Stocks?

A penny stock is a company stock (or share) that has a value under $5 and that is usually traded over-the-counter (OTC) through the OTC Bulletin Board (OTCBB) and pink sheets. On rare occasions, you will find some NYSE or other standard companies trading under $5 per stock. Unlike the main stock exchange traded penny stocks, most OTCBB traded penny stocks are highly volatile due to their low value and hard maneuverability including wide ranged bid-ask spreads and small capitalization.

As I stated, most penny stocks are limited to the OTCBB. Few companies can be traded on main exchanges, such as the Nasdaq, with share values under $5. This does not make those companies "penny stocks" in tradability only in name since their capitalization and tradability are high and fluid.

The big difference between a standard stock company and an OTC penny stock company is in the filing process.

OTC penny stock companies only require a market maker to support their request:

1. Either contact FINRA or OTC Markets Group Inc. and request to register for trade.
2. Provide a Market maker (Broker) that sponsors the request.
3. The market maker will fill in form 211 on the FINRA or OTC MG site.
4. You are set for trade on the "Pink."

Standard stock companies are companies that make an initial public offering (IPO), which is the way all privately owned companies get traded on standard stock exchanges. An IPO is basically the process in which a company will try to raise funds to increase their credit and asset value to propel growth or to propel further research and development of a product before it gains access to a global market. All IPO's require specific preparations that include:

1. Forming an IPO team that includes an authorized underwriter, lawyers, Certified Public Accountants (CPA), and a Securities and Exchange Commission (SEC) expert.
2. The IPO team prepares a company profile with all the financials and projections. This prospectus is then circulated for public scrutiny.
3. An official team of experts audits the financial statements.
4. Filing its prospectus and financial statements with the SEC and schedule the public offering date.

As you can see, there is a very big difference between how a regulated standard IPO is processed and how penny stocks are processed for trade. In general, penny stock companies represent companies that have limited access to private venture capital and that are seeking a de-regulated source of income that can provide them with large quantities of capital and a more fluid and public environment to work in.

While it is rare to find lucrative companies traded with penny stocks, it is not unheard of to find a few emerging technologies start from a simple penny stock company and transferring to the mainstream stock exchanges. There is also a reverse function too, where companies that were traded on main stock exchanges fell into debt or became untradeable and were transferred to trading on an OTCBB.

Other ways that penny stocks become standard stocks are:

1. The company can set up a new IPO with the SEC or a regulatory body
2. If a company reports that they have more than 2,000 investors.
3. If a company has more than 500 uncategorized (non-accredited) investors with an asset value of over $10 million.
4. If the company has listed its securities with a national security exchange such as the NYSE or NASDAQ.

In many cases, you will find that companies with over $10 million in assets would prefer a proper listing rather than a penny exchange due to the transparent nature and fluidity of trade. This means that most of the penny stocks are split between companies that are not worth the time to trade in and companies that are worthwhile investing in since they will emerge with a new technology or business model (such as with the gig economy) and require the IPO to raise the initial capital they could not get through private investors or financial institution loan channels.

A Brief History of Penny Stocks

Penny stocks have been around since companies started to trade their shares. In fact, they have been traded on all exchanges since the first exchange opened for trade (not the first exchange to open) in NY (the NYSE) in 1817, followed by the London Stock Exchange that opened in 1801 but only started to trade in 1825.

The concept of valuing a company is a standard issue of market competence, the number of shares a company will offer to investors is not standard. The reason behind penny stock value is based on two models of thought:

Cheap Loans
Expectation of Growth

The first model is the most acceptable one, where a company will value itself and then issue shares valued at one cent each, this will automatically create a lot of shares, this allows for a more flexible approach to investing. The cheaper the stock and the larger number available is one way of attracting many investors with small amounts to invest, such as $100. Once a company has raised a sufficient amount of capital, it can leverage the capital for a bank loan or credit line.

The second model strategizes the future where the cheap share will grow exponentially, inviting more investors as the stock meets its milestones and grows in value. This approach generates speculation and stock prices can fluctuate based on the perception of market status. This second approach is sometimes used to attract serious investors, institutions that want a regulated company, even if it is only lightly regulated.

The Bubbles in Time

The over speculation of penny stocks fueled the 1929 US stock market crash. They were the major factor in the crash, where a lot of small companies were pushed up in value until the balloon burst. This led to the creation of the Securities Exchange Act of 1934. This Act came to regulate penny stocks, limiting their cap to $3 (Changed later to $5) and restricting their trade away from main stock exchanges.

Another change came to the penny stock market in 1990, with the Penny Stock Reform Act that was born out of a need to regulate the market due to too many fraudulent manipulations. The House Committee on Energy and Commerce determined that:

1. There was a lack of public information that allowed brokers and dealers to manipulate trades.
2. Too many promoters and other people associated with marketing penny stocks were offenders of security laws and even convicted felons or had links to organized crime.

This led to the rules of transparency that make manipulation and fraudulent marketing harder and created the electronic trading platform that we know as the OTCBB.

Famous Penny Stock Companies

Monster Beverage Corporation (MNST): While it was founded back in 1935, this company was traded as low as $0.69 in 1995, and then in 2003 the energy drink market exploded, and Monster became a $68 stock value today.

Quality Systems (QSII): This company was founded in 1974, it developed a technology that few appreciated and less understood. They started to trade after an IPO in 1982, for most of the time it was traded around the $1 mark, and then in 2002 its technology was fully understood. It now trades around $13.

Mylan N.V. (MYL): This company's stock started out as a penny stock in 1973, transferring to the NYSE where it traded for under $5 for a while. In 2008 it moved to the

NASDAQ and now the company has a value of around $16.9 billion and a stock price of around $46.

An Introduction to OTCBB

OTCBB is an electronic trading platform set up by the National Association of Securities Dealers (NASD) as a response to the Penny Stock Reform Act of 1990, which directed the SEC to set up an electronic quotation and trading system for stocks that could not be traded on the standard stock exchanges such as the NYSE or the NASDAQ. Companies traded on the OTCBB do not need any listing requirements.

The platform provides a place where penny stocks can be listed, providing investors and speculators a location for performing up-to-the-minute quotes, receiving last-sale prices and volume information for equity securities traded over the counter (OTC). Company stocks traded on the OTCBB have the suffix ". OB" and trade is made between individuals, creating a focused supply and demand market. Trades are made by standard communications, and most OTCBB trades are not automated or have "bots" and algorithms to move them, due to their static nature.

The OTCBB is an important platform for the US economy. It provides many companies the chance to raise funds, giving the company a chance to develop into a larger company for a future main stock exchange IPO. The OTCBB is not an actual stock exchange; it is a managed through membership platform in a secure network of market makers that provide the public access to make trades.

Pink Sheets

This term refers to the daily list of ask and bid prices of penny stocks traded on the OTCBB. The reason they are called pink sheets is that they are printed on pink colored paper. If you come across this term, it merely suggests that the asset under discussion is an asset traded over the OTC.

Blue Sky Law

You might come across this terminology when researching and trading in stocks and options. Blue Sky refers to a state-specific law that regulates the trade of securities in a specific state. These are in addition to SEC and NASD requirements placed on dealers and brokers. Blue sky laws are additional state laws to protect investors from fraud. The term "Blue Sky" comes from an early source that was referred to by U.S. Supreme Court Justice Joseph McKenna in the Supreme Court case on the constitutionality of state security laws; Hall v. Geiger-Jones Co., 242 U.S. 539 (1917), McKenna stated "speculative schemes which have no more basis than so many feet of 'blue sky'".

What are the SEC rules for Penny Stocks?

The SEC and the Financial Industry Regulatory Authority (FINRA) set specific rules regulating the trading of penny stocks. All broker-dealers must comply with Section 15(h) of the Securities Exchange Act of 1934 and any accompanying rules.

§240.15g-9
Sales Practice Requirements

- All transactions must be approved by the broker-dealer (BD).
- The BD customer must sign a written agreement to represent each trade.
- Every BD will have a customer "Approval" process that includes all the necessary documents and proof of identity for a BD before allowing customer access to trading on the OTCBB.

- The approval of a customer will only be granted after the customer has also provided proof of trading experience and the trading objectives.

Translation: When you open a trading account you will have to fill out various online forms that provide the BD with your name, address, and legal citizenship status. You will also have to answer some basic questions, such as: Why do you want to invest? You will be given a few answers to choose from. All applicants must provide a scanned copy of a personal identification document and proof of address.

§240.15g-2
Disclosure Document

All BD's must provide online a disclosure document for the customer to read and understand.

The document must include the following information:

- The risk factors in penny stock trading over the OTCBB
- Concepts and fundamentals of penny stock trading
- The customers right's
- The BD's responsibilities and duties to the customer
- How the BD will remedy, and damage was done to the customer due to OTCBB fraud and other activities that might affect the customer's holdings

Translation: It is worthwhile and important to read any disclosure document when trading over the internet. You might find significant differences in the responsibilities of BD's to their customers, and a lot of "shady" brokers will have a lot of unusual and ambiguous clauses which you don't want to accept. Also take note of how much, and how the BD charges fees.

§240.15g-3
Bid-Offer Quotations Disclosure

Broker-Dealers must provide accurate, and up to the moment trade prices before any transaction can be placed. Transparency of trade is of key importance to the OTCBB.

§240.15g-4
Compensation Disclosure

This disclosure is key to understanding your profit margin. Some brokers can take a very large fee or create a spread that can minimize your chances of quick trades. It also tells you how much you must pay per trade, which is key to understanding how the BD makes its profits. Different fees and methods can determine whether the platform is "greedy," something to make all potential customers wary.

§240.15g-6
Monthly Accounts Statements

Once you have started to trade, the BD must record all trades and send you a monthly report. The report will include the following details:

- The name and number of each stock traded
- The name and number of each stock in the customer's account
- The dates of each translation within the monthly report period

- The purchase price and the estimated market value of the stock.

The monthly statement must also include an explanation of the stock's market limits and an estimation of the stock's price in the market. However, if a customer's account has been inactive for over six months, then the BD exempt from sending a monthly report.

Summary

The SEC does not regulate penny stocks as they do for standard companies traded on the main stock exchanges. There is no mandatory requirement for information, which is why only the Broker-Dealers should be considered as platforms for investment. Broker-Dealers are basically brokerage companies that provide a platform for customers to trade in penny stocks for a fee. As you can see, there are very limited regulations in place, which makes trading in penny stocks a highly speculative game. Most exchanges offer various tools to gauge market movements and provide insights (news) into stocks being traded. However, due to the nature of this market, a lot of the news must be viewed with speculation as well and cross-referenced to assess the credibility of the information.

The Four Penny Stock Levels

Traditionally penny stocks mean a stock that is valued around $0.01, (a penny or a cent) however the SEC defines a penny stock as having a market value under $5.00, and this literally means under $5.00. You will find four penny stock category levels, these are:

1. Above $1.00
2. Between $0.01 and $0.99
3. Between $0.001 and $0.099
4. Between $0.0001 and $0.0099

Yes, you got it right the first time! Penny stocks can trade for as low as one-thousandth of a cent. You might usually see such fractions when trading in Forex or cryptocurrencies (Bitcoin etc.) however, company stocks can also be traded at such low values too. As one mathematician once told me, don't let the 0's confuse you, they are all numbers on a page, look at the trading range, at the company metrics and watch out for scams. Now, let's look at the difference between each level.

The Dollar Penny Stocks: $1.00 - $4.99

These really defeat the object of the exercise, since they trade in similar levels to some main stock exchange papers. The first thing you should look at is the company's history. Check out how long it has been trading, where it was and what is its future. Any company trading above $1.00 is either a serious contender for a future IPO or aiming to transfer to the main exchanges. On the flip side, it could be a company that was once big and failed and has no future. Any stock traded above $1.00 will only be traded in values of up to one penny increments, this means that trades will never move from two decimal places.

Traditional Penny Stocks:
$0.01 to $0.99

These are the traditional version of a penny stock, where the value of the stock trades between one cent to under a dollar. Some companies stock trade in these values on the NYSE and other main markets, but they are given fair warning from the SEC that if their stock value does not go over $1.00, they will be moved to the OTC. Stocks under $1.00 can be traded to values of four decimal places, or up to a thousandth of a dollar.

Hundredth Penny Stocks:
$0.001 to $0.099

There is no real difference between this and the next group; it is just an easy way to categorize different stocks. The lower the stock value, the lower the company's tradability and value. Basically, these are companies that have no intrinsic attraction to investors, unless an investor happens to know what the company's future looks like.

The Triple Zero Stocks:
$0.0001 to $0.0099

This is the subatomic world of manipulation. Where companies try to attract speculators and where manipulators still try to make 1000% profits in a day, every day. The incremental change of 0.001 is so small that major stockholders can show asset values that jump exponentially. However, while buying is easy, trading and selling are hard, and many of the news items and blog articles about these companies are often pushed by the very speculator that bought into the share.

The triple zero stock is not cryptocurrency nor a lottery ticket

Some people might make the mistake that a triple zero penny stock will act like a cryptocurrency, where slight movements are translated into hundreds of percents. This is not the case; triple zero stocks do not have the fluid mechanics of the cryptocurrency exchanges, they are not tradeable like bitcoin and in fact are the exact opposite. While their value might sometimes seem attractive, buying into a company for $1,000 to get 10% of its stock, is like buying lottery tickets with one difference, a lottery ticket is a binary option, you either win or lose and do so immediately. Triple zero stock is hard to move, even harder to move in large amounts and is invariably not holding any surprises. Triple zero is the domain of scammers. I would not invest in these unless the intent is to buy out a public company for a future secondary IPO.

Where to Trade in Penny Stocks?

The OTCBB is not one single exchange like the NYSE or the NASDAQ. It is a network of dealer-brokers linked together making trades. It is actually very similar to the blockchain theory but without the technology infrastructure. That is why penny stock trading is very similar to the cryptocurrency market and why bitcoin and other such coins have become so popular. However, unlike the volatile "get rich quick market" of cryptocurrency, the penny stock market is a slow market to get rich.

There are thousands of dealer-brokers online, in fact, every bank that offers stock trading accounts will give their client access to these markets. Private investment companies, dealers, and brokers, as well as online exchanges, are increasing in numbers every day due to the international demand and ease of access that the internet has produced.

The best place to get up to date information about any traded penny stock without bias is from the Financial Industry Regulatory Authority (FINRA) website: www.finra.org. Here you will find a list of all the penny stocks as well as their:

- individual current market quote,
- a list of stock options,
- the company profile,
- bond issues,
- financial status,
- key ratios,
- trading volumes,
- major shareholders,
- insider data about their executive board and management,
- company filings of their reports,
- stock performance,
- corporate actions, and

- industry peers (which companies are in the same * industrial/service category).

The FINRA site is the best place to gather unbiased data, and to then compare that data with researched information. How and where you research information is individual, however, it is best to use only recognized and reliable sources.

Trading will be done over a registered platform after you have completed the necessary application process and injected some cash into your trading account. Here is a list of some broker-dealers that you can choose from. Remember to check the application clauses, what fees you will pay per deal.

OTC Markets Group Inc.

https://www.otcmarkets.com

This company has set up a major OTC trading platform used by thousands of dealer brokers. You can go online and choose from any one of their listed customers. The site also provides insights and details of the various stocks traded. They have split their platform into three categories:

- OTC QX: A standard stock exchange platform, where companies are traded on an established public market.
- OTC VB: a focused stock exchange platform, where the most interesting venture capital start-ups are traded.
- Pink: The OTCBB penny stock platform, where all the penny stocks with limited data are traded.

The OTC markets Group is just one technology platform provider among many, but it does provide a comprehensive service to both dealer-brokers as well as to investors and speculators.

Here is a quick look at two alternatives, so you can compare the difference in approach to trading between competing for brokerage firms.

TD Ameritrade

https://www.tdameritrade.com

This is a dealer-broker site using a bespoke trading platform and that provides access to many financial markets including the OTCBB. It is a more expensive company to join, but it provides an excellent platform and data for research. Their drawback is the commission of $6.95 you pay per trade.

Interactive Brokers

https://www.interactivebrokers.com

This broker offers a free trading platform, with no fees from trades but you cannot open an account for less than $10,000. So, this broker is looking for serious volume, which is not the best solution for penny stock traders who want a small portfolio.

"Go Bespoke or go Broke."

Most trading account applications are generic, but most trading platforms are bespoke. This means that you will need to decide which trading platform is best suited to your trading and what is the site's GUI (Graphic User Interface). There is a lot of psychology and personalization in GUI and not every GUI is user-friendly to every use. I suggest you open up a number of trading accounts with different platforms and brokers, and then test them all with a trial (free) run. All serious companies offer test accounts. Once you find the GUI that suits your personal feelings and provides what you would call a quality trading with information experience. Then trade with that platform. Another issue with different brokers are the different assets they allow you to trade with since you will most probably not just deal in penny stocks, check out which platforms provide you with access to mainstream exchanges, forex and other assets such as commodities and cryptocurrencies.

Investor Awareness

I will state this warning a few times in this book, most brokers are ethical and serious people with an interest in earning money from successful trading. However, the world is rife with unethical people, and while there are rules and regulations that limit trade on penny stocks, there are no rules or regulations that guard investors against unscrupulous dealers and brokers. Since trading is a person to person activity with a brokerage platform in between, make sure you are working with a reputable firm, and even so, never rely 100% or even 50% on information they supply. Always double and triple check our information when it comes to penny stock trading data. Chapter 9 presents a classic example backing up my warning.

How to Trade in Penny Stocks

Trading in penny stocks is a speculative and sometimes dangerous occupation. You can literally lose your investment, or in a slightly better or worse scenario (depends on how you look at it) get your money stuck in a company that has no trading volume and you cannot sell your holdings.

Before you start trading in penny stocks you should read, know and understand these four facts:

Penny Stock History and Information

Penny stock companies are not required to provide all the information that regulated stocks are required to provide by law. This means that "knowing" what you are invested in is limited. Before you invest in a really cheap stock with the "hope" it will make you a millionaire overnight, check the company behind the ticker symbol. The history of the company is as important as the updated market data is for reaching an informed decision. There are several ways to gain information, and they include the use of internet data sources as well as ground-level information. You must compartmentalize all your information into three categories:

- **Official sources:** FINRA, SEC, State and official local sources (County and City information). You can also checkup company tax filings. Official sources are not biased (or should not be!); they report only what they see. You will get no other insights or opinions, only hard facts, and figures.
- **Reliable sources:** CNN, BBC, other major news services, professionals that know the company or are in the same

sphere that the company is involved in, universities and research articles. Some news services are also unreliable since news has been known to be manipulated for personal reasons. So, just be careful, never rely on one source, always cross check with at least three news services and make sure that one has not copied the content and re-written it from the other, which is a well-known trick in modern online news reporting.

- **Unreliable sources:** social or business media sources are usually an unreliable source since the content is bias based and therefore cannot be ascertained as impartial or reliable. However, you can check by asking in forums online and read up on the discussion. If you are close to the company's physical address, you should ask around locally if people have heard about the company, but in most cases you will not live nearby. However, in any case, don't get pulled into believing word of mouth or hearsay, wherever the information comes from.

No Minimum Standards

The OTCBB does not require any minimum standard of compliance. This means that anyone that has successfully passed an IPO can be traded on the OTCBB. While this might seem a good base to start from, it is not. Some companies were deregulated from a major exchange to the OTCBB due to financial problems, and other successfully raised funds in an IPO and ended up being traded once a month only, or in small increments of under $1 a day. Due to the lack of a minimum standard, the fluidity and reliability of trading are limited.

Stock Liquidity

This is really where the crunch is. Most of the penny stocks traded are static. Before you start to trade in penny stocks, check what the history of their tradability. Also, check how much of the company's holdings are traded. If you find a company that is trading less than 50% of its stock, then you are basically in the hands of the company's owners. If you find a company that has over 65% of its stock traded, then you are at the mercy of the market. However, there is an upside, if you want to buy a traded company, which is what many companies try to do to get immediate access to an IPO, buy out a penny stock company and use its OTCBB status to bypass the need for an initial IPO.

If, however, you are a standard trader or inquisitive speculator, then you must check the fluidity of the stock in question. Make sure that you can sell after you buy. There is no gain in buying a penny stock for thousands of dollars and then trying to sell it for millions when no one is buying it because everyone knows it's a pumped-up price. This process is called "pump and dump" and is the main reason behind the Penny Stock Reform Act of 1990's.

Trading Hours

The OTCBB works all hours, which means you can post trades 24/7, since trades are made P2P, if another person is online and willing to buy the stock, or puts in an ask to your bid, then your stock will be traded. It is important to check out the after-hours trading prices. You will be surprised by the number of trades that occur after normal US hours. This is due to the international nature of the stock as well as certain individuals and brokers relying on the fact that the majority of penny stock investors are inexperienced and will think that the market closes for the night. Many "pump and dump" scenarios have played out overnight. However, due to the personal nature of the penny stock market, where 'bots' are not used due to the constraints of these markets, most trades are low volume. Which means, even if your holdings jump from $10 to $10,000, you won't be able to sell them, and as you try, so will everyone else, causing the prices to fall back to or even below $10.

Trading Tips

The first thing to remember is that the market is static, low volume and volatile. Which means it's like gambling on a 1c roulette table, where the wheel turns once an hour. If you think you will get rich quick, think again. If you are willing to take risks and try to earn a lot of income on a yearly basis, then this might be the market for you.

The key is finding where the movers are occurring. It's a bit like the heat maps in the Uber driver's app, where surges of customer saturation lead drivers to rush and pick up passengers. You must be able to notice the signs that lead a company stock into a surging stock. This means that something or someone is moving the market, and you need to act quickly.

Get in on the ground floor and sell in the middle. Set your profit percentage and don't be swayed by greed. This means that if you can enter a surging stock, set your profit spread, and stick to it. A penny stock trader is in for the short game; there are no long holdings here unless you know of a tech company that will emerge in a years' time. Sort of like investing in Apple shares back in 1976 as a small private investor, when the company just started out and then waiting 20 years to be worth a few billion. Not everyone is ready to do that, and honestly, the OTCBB is not really the place for that.

The Golden Rule or Master Tip

If you are seeking a get rich quick scheme go to a casino or do cryptocurrencies, stock markets are not the place for you. If, however, you are seeking an informed speculative decision-making process that can lead to riches, then penny stocks are the place to be.

Tip #1: In the US, Restrict Yourself to the NYSE & NASDAQ

Yes, this might sound like an oxymoron, but check out the company's history. If this company is not going down due to bankruptcy, then I would invest hard. The best example I can give was AIG when it crashed, and investors bought in at $2 a share. The premise was that AIG is too big to go under, and that premise was true. The government stepped in, and after a year, AIG stock was being traded at $32 a share. It is now being traded around $64. This means that for every $1,000 investment back in 2009, one year later in 2010 you would have $16,000 (sounds like Bitcoin but better!). Before investing in a penny stock on these exchanges, make sure you are fully informed of its history and direction. You don't want to hold onto a stock that will be deregulated to the OTCBB.

Tip #2: Go International

Don't just restrict yourself to two markets, check out global stock exchanges in Europe and Asia. There are many penny stocks being traded on major markets, all you need to do is research them to understand their potential. Before you go jumping onto the FTSE or the Tōshō, check out what rules and taxes apply to you as a foreign investor. Also, just as with any US market, check the credibility of the company you are investing into. Make sure you only take your information from reliable sources, do not invest in a company that has been "promoted" or been given as a "hot tip." There are a lot of international scams going around, especially with US offshore companies.

Tip # 3: Suspect Every News Source

Don't let the hype pump your expectations. When it comes to penny stocks, make sure you read every news source and cross check everything. Unlike AIG in 2009, most penny stocks are not corporate giants. They will not be saved from chapter 11. You must make sure you invest in sound companies. Even when trade is static, a sound company will not lose its value overnight. Also, do not believe bombastic sales pitches from unreliable online sources. You will find sites suggesting the next new "Microsoft" or "Uber" stock. This is often coming from an investor with a heavy position in the stock seeking a patsy to buy it up at the pumped price or to create a pumped price, so they can unload their position.

Tip #4: Volume is King

Volume means Fluidity, and that means a company is alive. However, read the news and make sure you understand the scope of the expected fluidity. For instance, back in the 80's, there were many oil exploration companies coming along and selling penny stocks. You could buy up 10% of a partnership for under $10,000. This was the age of oil exploration fever, and any company posting it had found oil, cause their stock value to rise by 10-20 times their value, with crazy volumes daily. If you can spot these stocks, then buy in and be prepared to watch the market 24/7. You should either set a profit cap, such as 100% or 200% as a profit cap or a time cap, where you can decide to sell within 24 or 48 hours, cashing out on the immediate activity. Another issue with volume is how much of the volume you trade with. Limit yourself to under 10% of the daily volume, don't get caught in the trap that you are the market maker. It means you are buying more than you can sell. Keeping your volume around the 10% mark means you can buy and sell daily.

Tip #5: Learn to Trade Not Gamble

There is a big difference between trading and gambling. Trading is when you buy and sell assets based on informed decisions. Gambling is when you take a chance on a situation occurring as you expect it to, or based on a gut instinct. Set limits to your trading, remember the profit percentage rule, and never leave it. Always follow a rigid mental approach to penny stock trading. Otherwise, you will end up with a lot of paper and no cash. The profit cap rule should be conservative, don't limit yourself to a 1:1 profit or even a 1:2 profit margin. Set it to a 5:1 profit limit per trade. Taking a 20% profit is better than losing your investment, as the saying goes, "a bird in the hand is better than two in a bush."

Another factor in trading that separates it from gambling is knowledge. Knowing the history, the market and understating the company you are investing into. Knowledge is power, and you can easily check up on the company's financials by looking at three key factors:

- **Institutional Investors**: the higher the percentage of holdings held by financial institutions, the stronger the asset. With penny stocks, you won't find high percentages, but if you find companies with zero institutional investors, be aware that you are investing in an untested or unwanted stock. Even when there are institutional investors, as this is the case with some hi-tech companies, do not charge in and buy without checking the company information and market data first.

- **Trading Volume**: We already discussed this, the volume is a key indicator of the tradability, fluidity, and overall popularity of the stock. With penny stocks, trading volume is erratic, when you see a sudden spike or surge, this is the time to sell, not buy. So, don't buy immediately, unless the market analytics that you assessed show you that the company is not in a spike, but in an exponential rise to success.

- **Floated Shares**: The higher this number, the lower the value of the stock. Essentially the volume of floated shares can be anywhere from a million to a trillion. Unless you are Microsoft or Apple, having a billion stocks will not make your paper price go up to $1, it will most probably trade around the $0.0001 mark. The bottom line is; check what the potential market price can reach by looking at this value.

These three key factors will give you the basic information that turns a gamble into risky speculation or even to a calculated investment.

A word about Gut Instinct, this is a very important tool to listen too, if you know that your gut instincts have proven to be correct in the past. In this case, listen to your gut, but only after you have researched your position and understood the market, the company, and as much of the jibber-jabber that is coming from unreliable sources.

Tip #6: Hit, Run, and Retain

The best way to maximize profits in a penny stock is to hit and run, going in for the quick kill when the chance arrives. However, some investors like to take out their initial investment amount plus a profit and leave in a percentage for the long-term chance. For instance, if you have a trade that brings you in 100% profit, you would sell between 50% to 75% of your holdings, this gives you either a stop-loss break even with a small profit and allows you the peace of mind to check out the future of the stock. This system allows you to take the "small profit" or "incremental profit" approach and secures your funds from high-risk losses. Just remember that some positions will give you a 20-40% spread, sell, don't wait. If you get such an opportunity, make the run, and continue to the next trade. It sometimes pays to keep a small amount invested in the penny stock after you cashed out with a profit. Retaining small amounts of stocks can add up over time, giving you an interesting portfolio for future trading.

Tip #7: Focused Trading

Focused trading is concentrating on one stock at a time. By focusing your attention on one stock that is entering a volume curve that suits your investment model will enable you to get in and out of trade within one day, sometimes allowing you to make a few trades with small amounts daily. These small amounts add up, and you will find that you are making thousands of dollars a month from many small day trades, where each profit margin can be anywhere from $10 to $1,000. A profit is a profit, no matter how small it is and profits in a penny market should be in penny levels, meaning, adding small amounts on a daily basis, creating a large monthly profit.

Remember, it does not matter whether you are invested in Boeing or in Bling, the numbers that the penny stock price represent still stand behind one corporate entity. The company is what you are investing in, try to not be drawn into investing in ten penny stocks because they are so cheap, the amount of time you will need to invest in maintaining an informed decision, as well as overlapping trades, will be enough to take your mind off reaching a truly comprehensive understanding of each decision. In one sentence "Don't spread yourself too thin."

Tip #8: Ignore all Success Stories

Ignore anyone that tells you he or she became a penny stock millionaire, offering you some penny stocks to invest in as a tip. These are scammers seeking to "pump and dump." These tips usually come into your e-mail or as feedback in blogs and social media sites. The only success story will be the one where you are offered tips and insights into trading successfully without giving you names of stocks to trade in. Success stories will always be backed up with successful stocks, which means that if the company is truly successful, then the stock won't be an OTCBB penny stock. However, it is easy to check out success stories, just look at the news, and see how "popular" the company really is in a simple Google search. Also, do not fall for the "peer review" journal approach, there are many biotech and medical device companies that try to promote their "success" through published articles. These articles do not promote success, they only promote research. Success comes from regulated authorizations, such as an FDA level being accomplished, and believe me, if the FDA does publish a company success at one stage, the whole investment world will be buzzing about it.

Tip #9: Be Wary of Company Management

If you do decide to trade on the OTCBB, then just be wary of everyone, especially the company. In most cases, companies traded on the OTCBB will try to find ways to pump up their value for credit reasons. Where company trading value is an indicator for banks and other financial institutions that give these companies credit and loans for operational purposes. Also, don't fall in love with a company you are invested into even if it is the next autonomous vehicle messiah, unless SoftBank invests in it as well. Treat all stocks the same, as tools and opportunities to make a profit, not as a virtual lover to stroke your ego. Remember that many company's owners and executives will do anything they can to make their companies market value go up, and that includes making promising projections of the company's future without backing the projections with facts. Hi-Tech (especially medical device and bio-research) development companies are famous for doing this.

Tip #10: Don't Trade in Shorts

Keep your trading simple; a quick get in and out. Penny stocks are too volatile for shorts, and if there is a pumped-up stock, check why it's pumped up. Shorts are a great tool for fluid markets such as forex. They are not good for the OTCBB. There is only one exception to this rule, and that is for experienced traders only, it is called hedging your position, and comes when an investment is put in a speculative stock, and a short is set for a specific target. The calculation is that the profit from the short will offset the loss of a failed investment as much as the profit from a successful investment will overshoot the loss from the short position.

Risks and Manipulations

Let's take a look at market manipulations, at the various "criminal" schemes used to manipulate penny stocks and at the investors seeking to make a quick killing on this market.

First of all, schemers and scammers are banking on an investor's greed to overcome their common sense. Greed makes people stupid and they end up discounting all warning signs. Most of them end up moaning and crying foul, when in fact they were the real culprits and not the scammers. Criminal elements are always around, it's part of human nature, so it is up to the smart investor to be prepared and not fall into the trap of their own greed and avarice.

The Pump and Dump Scheme

This is the classic scheme, it happens all the time, and it is up to you to ignore the crap and concentrate on the real news. Pump and dump campaigns are usually bombastic and wild claims for a specific stock's future, and why you must invest in them now. These are schemes to get as many people to invest in the stock, pushing prices up and allowing the scammers to prepare for a big sell-off. Pump and dump promotions are paid for adds, or direct social media postings, at worst spam messages.

The Short-and-Distort Scheme

This is found at the end of a successful pump and dump scheme, where the stock price has been pushed up to wonderous proportions. Now the scammer has pumped up the market or has watched a market get pumped. He buys up shorts and starts to pump the market with negative news to instill panic and fear, making the investors sell at any price they can to save whatever cash they can get out of the stock.

Mining Scams

As I mentioned above, when oil exploration was a hit in the 80's and 90's, so too was mineral mining, especially gold. This swindle has one difference from real mining or exploration shares. These scammers deal in falsifying information. The basics are that a company will set itself up, make an IPO raise cash for a mining purpose, or perhaps make a "reverse merger" where they buy out a dead penny stock company and use its framework to make another IPO (a second IPO is much easier than making an initial IPO).

The company then starts feeding the market with false claims of impending finds. Speculators start to invest heavily, and then when the truth comes out, they find that the company's initial investors have already cashed out, leaving a dead and worthless shell.

Guru Scams

What can be said that has not already been said about Gurus? They float on air and talk to the God's of their ancestors and tell you that your soul was once a Nile Princess or famous Roman Caesar. Which is interesting, since out of billions of previous lives, the only ones that seem to come back are Nile Princesses and Roman Officials; nobody seems to come back from being a clothes washer in Calcutta.

These amazing Gurus, use their virile intelligence and mystical abilities to suggest high profit-making tips. Of course, you have to pay them high fees for their mystical insights. The best way to deal with "read my book to get rich in 30 seconds" is to trash the mail and move on to more important issues.

"No Net Sales" Schemes

This is basically a trader scam, where the brokerage or trader will tell a client that they have to buy a specific stock for a long time period. Hold onto it, and such like rubbish. This is one of the worst scams around because it requires an actual broker or dealer to make the pitch, and the unsuspecting client will listen and follow orders. If you encounter such an issue, contact the SEC immediately, don't try to contact the brokerage firm owners, since you don't know how far up the scam goes. Just aim for the jugular and send an immediate request to the SEC to investigate the brokerage.

The Risks of Hi-Tech

If you intend to invest in a hi-tech or venture capital company that offers you an amazing product that will take over the world next year, consider all the sources you must view. Hi-tech is a sector that can be easily rated. There are so many sources of information online, and science is exact. The product is not the issue in hi-tech companies; it's the marketing that counts. There are some amazing companies developing some leading-edge technologies, and they have crap marketing and PR, leading them to oblivion and obscurity. At the same time there are some companies producing mediocre technologies that vie for a place in the market, but due to wonderful marketing and PR, advance to the top of the ranking boards, attracting interest and accumulating value.

Let's look at some unknown companies that became obscure and eventually closed down, even though they had leading edge technology well before their competitors even arose.

PsiOS: Newsnet developed a website program to help you build your own website. Their core was so flexible you could basically open up every kind of business online, from blog to e-shop and from casino to e-bay trading platform. The mechanics were amazing. The help was unbelievable, and the company managed to publish it in 8 languages. It had over 500,000 websites online when it closed. The company invested in development and did not concentrate on marketing. It never raised the capital to make it big. Just for general knowledge, there are still no companies that offer the PsiOS flexibility that was created back in... 2004!

SideCar: The first rideshare company that came before Uber was Sidecar, a California based company that developed the first rideshare app and business model. It managed to survive till 2015 when the State of California put a stop to operations by implementing the TNC rules. Uber and Lyft managed to survive the transfer, but SideCar did not. There is an argument that Wingz started before sidecar. However, it is a moot point since also Wingz is an obscure service.

Bottom Line

Knowledge of the market is not enough, understanding what the market means is what completes the picture. The above examples were taken to show you that understanding the market mechanics also means understanding the nature of the hi-tech companies behind penny stocks. Believing in the technology is not as important as believing in the capability of the company to market their technology and business correctly. So when you come across a penny stock of a hi-tech company, check out how long it is on the market, go to "crunchbase.com" and check out how much investment they have and if they have serious backers (not that this helped SideCar), and check out their marketing history, which means check out who the main competition or leading tech company is in the same field.

An Example of Penny Stock Fraud

There are many examples of penny stock frauds and online scams. I chose this one as an example only because of its simplicity. Simplicity in duping investors, it was complex in set-up and required a lot of collaboration from unscrupulous brokers. Therefore, I always strongly state that even when getting information from brokers, check and cross-check to make sure. Brokers are just like anyone else, but with one difference, they trade with other people's money (OPM), and as the name suggests, some get "hooked" on other people's money and take advantage (just like Bernie Madoff).

In this case, it was Izak Zirk de Maison, a California based merchant banker. He devised a plan that involved setting up dummy corporations as penny stock companies, only since the IPO's were much quicker and easier than with standard IPO's. This meant that de Maison relied on partners in many brokerage firms around the country to help promote his dummy companies as a viable investment to unsuspecting investors. His operation started in 2008 and lasted for 5 years when he was apprehended by the FBI in 2013.

All the companies that de Maison created were reported as reputable firms involved in lucrative businesses such as gold mining in South America, global diamond trading and other commodity mining and trading. He also distributed stocks to all his collaborators, and then he set up an e-presence to give each company some meat. The companies included Kensington Leasing, Ltd., Lenco Mobile, Casablanca Mining, Ltd., Lustros, Inc., and Gepco Ltd.

Under fictitious names, de Maison would create executive boards, company CEOs and of course take personal stock in these companies under false names as well. He would then pump the price up with a classic "pump and dump" process. The only reason he was so successful was that he had brokers backing his scam. The reliance an investor places on a broker is misplaced, and that is what de Maison was backing on.

De Maison backed up his infrastructure with boiler room support, where salespeople call up and apply pressure to potential investors to take a position in the company's stock. Once the cast had been set, the stock values would start to rocket, and then de Maison and his cohorts would fulfill the ask volumes, as well as craftily balance bid quotes to maintain the pumped-up prices even further. At a specific point, he would dump the shares causing the prices to crash. De Maison had already cashed out enough on each deal, leaving the investors with worthless stock in an empty company.

Now brace yourselves, de Maison and eight accomplices managed to accumulate $54 million in sales!

The FBI field office in Cleveland received complaints about an Ohio based financial consultant that was being accused of fraud. This led the team to investigate the case. After reviewing all the evidence, a paper trail was a fund that let to de Maison and eight accomplices and eventually to their arrest and conviction. He was convicted in 2015 and sentenced to years in federal prison for committing securities fraud.

As you can see, penny stocks can be worth millions even when they are really worthless! Just like cryptocurrencies.

You can find this specific case information on the FBI website, and there are plenty more examples where this comes from. This article supports the unfortunate proposition that a sucker is born every minute.

In the words of the famous W.C.Fields: **"It's morally wrong to allow a sucker to keep his money."**

Conclusion

Trading in penny stocks is like trading in any other stock. It requires vigilance against scams, knowledge of the company that you want to invest in and an understanding of the market mechanics that govern the trade of the asset.

What I can tell you are the ten commandments of trading in penny stocks (assets):

1. Trading in any paper/digital asset requires a basic understanding of the market mechanics.
2. You must have access to reliable data on any asset's executive and history.

3. You must be properly informed of all the trading aspects before choosing a platform and broker.
4. You must invest only with the money you have.
5. Never take a loan to invest.
6. Always set a 30% cap on your cash assets to invest in speculative markets.
7. Do not trust any unreliable source.
8. Do not fall in love with an investment asset.
9. Do not deal in shorts or binary options on paper assets.
10. Hedge your position if you decide to disregard the first nine commandments.

It is obvious that everyone will develop their own investment technique, there are so many to choose from. However, the basics are identical in all. Knowledge of the market and the asset you intend to invest into are key to making an informed decision. The rest is up to you, whether you succeed in making a profit, buying into the right penny stock at the right time and selling it at a profit come down to your own actions and not the markets mechanics.

The only real variable in any successful investment is the investor and not the asset.

**If you have enjoyed this book, I would like to ask you if you would be kind enough to leave a review on Amazon.
It really helps us bringing more great books.**

Thank you and good luck.

Check Out My Other Books

Below you'll find some of my other books that are popular on Amazon and Kindle as well.

Dividend Stocks: How to Invest in Dividend Stocks to Maximize Your Return and Grow Your Portfolio Whether the Market Goes Up or Down

Passive Income: Simple Ideas to Start Earning a Passive Income Today to Add Some Money in Your Bank Account or to Change Your Life

Look for these titles on the Amazon!

Preview of "Dividend Stocks: How to Invest in Dividend Stocks to Maximize Your Return and Grow Your Portfolio Whether the Market Goes Up or Down"

Compounding

If you intend to invest in dividend stocks, then you should also learn a bit about compounding. This is the process by which you increase your direct profitability or your ROI from a specific dividend paying share. Due to the fact that dividend-paying companies tend to be financially stable and, in many cases, global companies, investing in them is usually a good idea - even without the dividend payouts. In most cases, these companies tend to increase in value over time, so there is a double profit made when investing in them.

Compounding in stock or cash dividends is actually quite common. A lot of investors seek out dividends to increase their holdings and their profits by investing in solid companies that have a proven track record of accomplishment for continuous growth. Such large global entities exist, and they provide a constant growth in stock value as well as a yearly dividend payout. Let's take the example of Coca-Cola, where the dividend payout in 2016 was $1.40 per share, and this increased to $1.48 in 2017. The share price also increased in between these years by an average of $3, from $40 to $43. While the value does fluctuate, there is a steady rise over time.

The general rule of thumb is that a constant dividend sharing company will likely continue to generate good ROI for its investors. Usually, these companies maintain a stable stock price and are healthier to invest in than companies that do not share their profits.

What is nice about dividend paying shares is the slow and solid performance they provide, day in and out, for investors. Young people starting families should consider portioning part of their monthly income and buying up such stocks, compounding the payout into buying more stocks of the same company with every payout. After 30-40 years, these investments will provide an exceptional pensions cushion.

The Compounding Power

Albert Einstein called compounding the "eighth wonder of the world." He was not wrong. There is definitely something wonderful about compounding income.

Compounding means adding the interest of one value back into the original value and then recalculating the value to give a new interest figure. In reference to dividends, this means that the return on investment or dividend payout will be reinvested into the original stock, either through buying more stock with the dividend money or gaining more stock with a stock dividend payout.

Just to get a taste of compounding, in an exaggerated way, I am going to show you the compounded accumulation of doubling. This means we always double the number we have and continue to do so for 30 days. In this instance, we will start with 1 cent.

...

Check out the rest of this book on Amazon!